LUMMOX Press

The
ACCIDENTAL
NAVIGATOR

New and Selected Poems

and a Story

By HENRY DENANDER

LUMMOX Press

ISBN 978-1-929878-88-8

First Edition

The Lummox Press
POB 5301
San Pedro, CA 90733-5301
www.lummoxpress.com

THANKS

The author wishes to thank Samuel Charters and Gerald Locklin
for their contributions over the years - I can't thank you enough
for your inspiration and support. Thank you Bill Roberts for
publishing my first books. Thanks also to the editors of the
following presses and magazines for publishing some of the poems
and the story contained herein: Bottle of Smoke Press, Artbureau,
Miskwabik Press, Chiron Review, Nerve Cowboy, Beggars &
Cheeseburgers, Poiesis, Rusty Truck, Pearl, Lummox Journal,
The Hold, Volta, Maintenant & remark.

For Marie & William

The Accidental Navigator
Table of Contents

Selected Poems

A Short Story

The
ACCIDENTAL
NAVIGATOR

New and Selected Poems
and a Story

Kryss on Denander

Two summers ago I was invited to give a talk to a group of students about my poetry. Difficult. So I began by reading a poem by d.a. levy. Then I threw a poem by Henry Denander out there. For the next two hours the talk consisted of reading some forty poems written by others, poems I admire and collect in a maple box under the bed.

It is no mistake that Denander's poems invoke this strong sense of ownership. A little like the fountain pen he presented to the world heavyweight champion. Denander's pen? It belonged to Johansson as well.

After taking in the Denander poem, the students sat there for a long moment, seemingly holding their collective breath. It was as if the champ himself had hit them in the breadbasket, in the gut.

The next response was just as instinctive—smiles broke out across the room. Even the instructor especially the instructor sat with a smile turned inward as if they had swallowed the truth and found it oddly palatable.

It was good to be there to see this. My reservations about the potential of words to produce even these changes in people were happily dismissed.

We know that a poem, once it is written, takes on a life of its own, and the person who wrote it fades into the woodwork. Each time my eyes glide down a page of this man I see someone completely unconcerned with any of this, who is just walking along and reporting. His poems have the warmth, good humor, and eye for the telling detail of the best correspondence; those letters we save in some place or other because they are too beautiful and necessary to lose.

—*Tom Kryss*

NEW POEMS

Beauty Sleep

I am sleeping with a CPAP,
it's a device that blows
air into my nose.

For years I've been snoring heavily and
suffered from sleep apnea.

With this tube attached to my nose
I no longer snore and I have a
good sleep.

But when I strap the mask on at night
my wife realizes I no longer look like
the handsome young man
she married

but more like Hannibal Lecter.

But I think she prefers
the Silence of the Lambs
to the Thunder in the Night.

Talking Tribeca #1

Twelve years ago in a
folk music club in Tribeca in NY,
I met the woman who's on the cover of
Bob Dylan's second album –
"The Freewheelin' Bob Dylan".

She was very beautiful back then
and was walking down the street
with her head on Dylan's shoulder.

When I met her it was a release party
for a new album by Dave Van Ronk,
and Suze Rotolo said hi when she
passed me and my friend.

When that album was released I was
just a young boy and she must have been
in her teens.

She was older now in Tribeca
but I was younger than her still.

...Henry Denander

The accidental navigator

Scientists in Spain now claim
it's not Christopher Columbus
who's buried in the
magnificient Sevilla cathedral

but his son;

there was a mix-up when the
remains were moved
in the 17th century.

Columbus discovered
America but we all know
he believed he'd actually
reached Asia.

And when he landed on Cuba,
he was certain
he was in Japan.

Now it seems he's lost
in Sevilla as well.

CBGB's (1992)

washing my hands
in the men's room
staring at those bright
graffiti walls and
the music from
the obscure Finnish band
22 Pistepirkko
loud and intense on stage
probably happy just
to be at this famous club
just as I was
washing my hands
in the men's room

one more beer and
the wall paintings
would be masterpieces
and the graffiti would turn
to poetry and my hands
would be dry for a firm grip
on another Rolling Rock beer

...Henry Denander

Fear of Flying

I pass the second hand bookshop on my
walk, and in the window I spot the bright
yellow paperback of Erica Jong's
"Fear of Flying".

I remember how I loved that book when
it came out in the late 70's; her open
sexuality, the outspoken story and
the *zipless fuck*.

When I return back home after my long walk,
I'm still thinking about that book and
if I should read it again.
I fumble with my keys and quickly try to

open the door. There are three different locks
and it takes a long time when I'm in a hurry;
now 30 years later I am more worried about
the *zipless pee*.

A softball game and the Murakami memory

Sometimes reading makes you remember odd things,
like when the Murakami short story about the
guy in school running straight into a board,
knocking himself out, made me think of a day at school
when I was a kid.

Our class had the afternoon off and my friend and I were
hanging out at the school yard. There was a class with girls
playing softball and suddenly their teacher asked us if
we wanted to play along.

We were thirteen years old and got embarrassed but also
proud to show off our talents for the girls. They used a small flat bat,
not the ordinary round stick we were used to and when it was my
time to bat I threw the ball up in the air and tried to hit it
the hardest I could, putting all my teenage strength
behind the bat, only to feel the bat slip out of my hand and fly
with an enormous speed straight over the heads of the girls,
hitting a basketball hoop on the next court with a really loud bang.

Afterwards, when the game was finished and my
blushing gone for good, I understood I could've killed one
of the girls with the flying bat.

Then I probably would've remembered it,
45 years later, even without the Murakami story.

...Henry Denander

It was like seeing a ghost walking the port of Hydra

My friend the American painter pointed him out to me, he was standing
with his back to us, wearing the kind of clothes that his father liked to use;
the blue and white T-shirt with the horizontal broad stripes and a pair of
black shorts. The hair short and cut just like his father's.

My friend greeted the entourage, made up of a wife and children and
grandchildren, and when Claude Picasso turned towards us it was
just like seeing the face of his father, the same profile, the same look.
We heard from our waiter that they are staying at Nikolaos, at
The Agius Hotel and that they stayed there for a month last year.

My wife thought it was a bit too much with the striped T-shirt, looking just like
his father, but I thought it was just right; that's the way I would do it if I was
Picasso's son and in charge of the estate.

Maybe though, I would stay two months instead - at that beautiful hotel
just down by the Nikolaos beach.

Dave Liebman at Fasching

The first time I saw Miles Davis in concert was in 1973 and Dave Liebman was in his band. 10 years later I was working for a Swedish record company that was recording Liebman. So when he was playing at a jazz club in Stockholm and no one from the creative department had time to go, I volunteered.

Liebman and Richie Beirach were there in their dressing room before the gig and I went to say hello. Liebman was wearing his trademark bandana and when he asked me if I had listened to the test pressings I was stunned since I didn't know about any test pressings and didn't know what to say. Liebman looked upset and told his partner, Hey he hasn't listened to the test pressings.

They thought I was a geek and I felt like one.

I listened to the gig and it was fine but I decided not to talk to them between the sets or after the gig. And I think they were just as happy about that.

I was new in the record business, later I got more professional and always said:

"- Yes, it sounds really good. Really good! This will be a classic record!"

But this time I was just a loser.

...Henry Denander

Nursing

When I came back from the hospital
I wanted to tell my son about what
they had done to me;

I'd suffered from a really painful
kidney stone and I had rushed
to the hospital to get it removed.

I told him there'd been one doctor and
two nurses present and I was about to tell how
they had performed a cystoscopy; by inserting a
long instrument through my very private parts
they had removed the stone from my bladder.

I told my 10-year old son
the nurses had started by cleaning
my "weenie".

William interrupted me:

- Did there really have to be *two* nurses to do that? he said

It was a good question.

At the racetrack

On eBay I bought four whisky glasses from
Santa Anita Park; this was Charles Bukowski's
favorite race track and he spent a lot of time there.

I've never betted on the horses myself but there was
a race track close to our summer house in Sweden
and I went there when I was a kid.

I never really liked to watch the horses run but
I came to see my uncle Allan who was a
regular at the track. I liked him a lot and he
always gave me money for ice cream,
so even without betting I came out ahead.

And now, 45 years later, here I am
with my large Santa Anita whisky tumbler
with the engraved horses and jockeys,
a couple of ice cubes and a large splash
of Glenlivet whisky.

Maybe I'm slowly
beginning to understand
the art of horseracing
after all.

...Henry Denander

One of us cannot be wrong

I am dreaming a lot, almost every night and last night I met Leonard Cohen at a square in Antibes, the small French town just outside of Nice, he was very kind and he remembered the book I'd sent him and of course we were in a way neighbours on the small island in Greece & he invited me up to the flat he was living in, and just outside the door to the steep steps up to the flat we met my old friend Åke, we couldn't believe it, what a coincidence and he's just as big a Leonard Cohen fan and he was stunned when he was invited to come up with us to the flat & soon Åke started to loosen up and when Leonard was trying to tell us something Åke interrupted him and started to tell old jokes and stories, Leonard was such a polite and friendly soul and he let him talk and smiled but in the end he took down his old guitar from the wall, the guitar that looked like the one from the cover of Songs From a Room, it was hanging there on the wall in his Hydra house with Marianne sitting over by the window & this room in Antibes looked much the same, all white and Leonard started to strum his guitar and even Åke got silent and suddenly Leonard started to sing and I thought what a fantastic moment this was and how I was sitting just close to Leonard and he was singing The Stranger Song with his characteristic rolling fingerpicking and then suddenly Åke started to sing along in a very loud and almost drunken-like voice and from there on my dream just went on and I couldn't really remember how it all ended, if it ever did, maybe they are still singing there in the room overlooking the quiet Place d'Antibe.

my wife shook hands with Muhammad Ali

that signed book is a special gift,
a gesture of love
she stands in line for hours
in a bookshop on Fifth Avenue

she doesn't know much about Ali
but when he stands up
he is huge

and when he thanks her for coming
his outstretched hand
is enormous

but for my wife
it's not the first time
she's held the hand
of a champ

...Henry Denander

Leaving the island

I dreamed I was about to leave the Greek island but I had already missed the boat several times. The Flying Dolphin took off outside from a long pier and I remembered how it once turned back and let us off because my friend had dropped his large leather bag in the water.

On the island we had met the painter Pablo Picasso several times, and he was there together with another well-known artist. I had pinched a small brochure from their yacht, and in there was a photo of Picasso that I wanted him to sign for me.

In the morning when we came down to the lobby of the hotel, I saw Picasso and his friend sitting just around the corner, with easels, painting on large canvases. At the same time we saw through the hotel's panorama windows that the Flying Dolphin was getting ready to leave. We rushed and packed our stuff, ran through the reception area with our bags and the large framed painting I had bought, and we stopped by Picasso to get his autograph. Picasso signed the back of the framed painting for me and at the same place he signed the name of his artist colleague and also the signature of Rembrandt. I realized it had been better if Picasso had just signed a photo for me, but there was no time.

My friend and I ran long the long pier and there were large spots where the cement was missing and we ran somewhat horrified on thin steel frames, seeing the water underneath. While running I remembered a scene from an old film where my friend was actually running over such iron grate, and it was a well-known scene from a classic black and white movie.

We managed to miss the boat again, and I suddenly felt drunk, and I was back in Stockholm and returning to The Opera Bar where I'd been earlier the same day. I was met by the manager Paulo who was very drunk and there was also Dan, the head waiter who now was extremely fat. He let us in to the bar where we met other waiters, all of them drunk. Paulo started to pour cognac down my throat from an enormously large bottle. One waiter was lying on the ground outside the back door.

I realized I had missed the boat, I was in a situation where I had a hard time finding my way. I didn't know where my luggage was and I had lost my coat.

workth

spamling your leaves
in tankards,

their waferly hands are
against our odds.

please,
please do not beg for
the door.

...Henry Denander

snooth

every night,

(before the small table strikes four):

the stirth of your arms are
at my gloth

and i am tuning my embranes
at the side of

you ear

lumpfs

wakened by all, but
much closer to each;

starting every new day
with these.

their November hands are not even -
but the rain is there,

always the
rain.

...Henry Denander

I found an old notebook from 1975 when I lived in Melbourne, Australia.

Peter Thomas and I used to play the Tatts Lotto at work every Friday. We filled in the form over the numerous beers we had with our lunch.

The week before I left Melbourne, we suddenly won 100 dollars and Peter said he'd send me my share to Sweden as soon as he'd received the check.

It's almost thirty years since I left Australia and his letter with the money still hasn't arrived.

I wonder what he's doing today, Peter Thomas. Is he still drinking half a dozen beers for lunch and then going back to work in the afternoon?

Now when everything's digital – is there still a separate room in every client's office for the telephone exchange? The place where we spent the best part of the afternoon, sleeping off the beers and hoping that our supervisor from Ericsson wouldn't show up?

Maybe you are retired now, Peter? Are you still catering for the army on Thursday nights?

I look forward to your letter, not so much for the money, but it would be good to hear from you.

The revenge of the couch potato

Zapping through the TV-channels
I stopped at Jeopardy, when I
recognized a familiar face from
35 years ago.

It was an old teacher I remembered
for his beard and his clogs.

He was a besserwisser and here he
was on prime time and I was sitting
on my couch watching him miss
almost every question.

At last he got what was coming to
him, Mr. Know-It-All.

I wish I could've been there in the
studio to tell him to do his lessons
better next time.

...Henry Denander

Jimmy Cobb at The Village Gate

Of all the great musicians from the Kind of Blue
recording in 1959, only Jimmy Cobb is still alive.

I saw him at The Village Gate in New York in
1992 and I have a vague memory of him being a
tough and mean drummer, not with the soft touch
he had on the Miles Davis album.

I recently found a box of old stuff from when I
lived in NY and there was a notebook with two
sketches I made of Jimmy Cobb at The Village
Gate.

On one of the drawings it said "Mean Jimmy
Cobb" and I had made horns on his head.

I remember seeing Elvin Jones once and <u>he</u> was a
mean drummer, but always smiling.

This mean drummer looked evil – but perhaps it
was just something he said at the gig or me being
drunk, late at The Village Gate.

Maybe he is a kind man
in the daytime.

We will not be staying for the entire performance

Freddie Hubbard was playing
at the Fasching Jazz Club
as a part of the Stockholm Jazz Festival.

We were tired after a long day of jazz and
tried to leave as quietly as possible,
passing the stage silently
so we wouldn't disturb the music.

Hubbard stopped playing
"Hey guys, are you leaving already?"

We smiled and waved but
already on our way through the door
we could hear him going on about us leaving.

For the rest of the set
the audience was
probably spellbound.

...Henry Denander

Royalty advances

He is a fantastic guitar and harmonica player and
has made records all over the world

and I was the financial guy at
a Swedish record company who had come to his hotel
to pay him his royalty advance.

I had his money in an envelope and
he counted the money once and smiled,
a really nice guy, his old hands shaking when
going through the dollar bills.

He counted the money again,
now really slowly and nervously,
putting note by note on his bed.

He was happy and we shook hands but
when I left, I saw him starting to
count the money again.

Later that year we recorded an album
with Chet Baker.

It was a Sunday afternoon and since
no one had told me he should be paid
in cash, I hadn't brought any money.

The recording was about to finish when
Chet told us he was leaving
really early next morning.

I realized we had to find some US dollars.

There was a Jazz Festival in Stockholm and
in the end we managed to borrow dollars from the
organizer.

We rushed back to the studio but
Chet had already left and
at his hotel they thought he could be
at the Italian restaurant down the street

There we found him, he had
just had his dinner and
was relaxing with a cup of coffee.

We didn't tell him our problems with the cash but
said we had been looking for him
to pay him his advance.

"Good", he said and
took the thick stack of dollar bills and
put them in his pocket
without
even looking at them.

...Henry Denander

Spies and bugging devices

I saw in the newspaper this morning
there is an exhibition at the
Swedish Army museum called "Spies"
with lots of interesting and strange stuff.

Among other things they are showing bugging devices
they found in the Swedish Embassy in Bucharest in the 80's.

My wife worked in the Embassy there at this time and
I remember how I laughed when I visited her and
she told me they expected that everything would be bugged,
even their own apartments.

And how they always went outside to talk if there was
something really important.

I laughed at her and thought they where overreacting;
it sounded too much like a James Bond movie to me.

OK, now they are showing the recorders and the
hidden microphones in the museum here.

Hopefully they haven't saved the recordings from
when I visited.

The Movie Star

I heard that Errol Flynn
tested almost everything;
booze, drugs and
both men and women.

Maybe it's true that
he gave his name to
the expression
"Trial and Errol"?

...Henry Denander

This poet

I have read quite a few poems by
this American poet, I like them all
and especially the way he ends
his narrative poems without a tag
and an obvious ending.
Everything's just hanging in the air
for you to catch.

I will try to do the same
and close one of
my prose poems without
my usual tag line.

Maybe in my next poem.

Stockholm Arlanda night shift

All through University I worked at the
Stockholm Arlanda airport, cleaning off
the outside of airplanes one night a week,
working in a cloud of strong-smelling cleaning
liquids that made us all tired and dizzy.

I had my lunch at 3 o'clock one morning and
went into the airplane to relax for 10 minutes,
in one of the passenger seats.

An hour later, when I suddenly woke up, the
airplane was moving and we were outside on
the runway. After the first few seconds of
panic, I realized the plane was being moved
by a truck.

Everyone laughed when I had to walk
all the way back to the hangar but
for once I was happy to get back to
the fumes again.

...Henry Denander

Botox

My neurologist tried a new cure for my never ending headaches; he injected ten shots of Botox into my skull.

Botox, in the undiluted form, is a very strong poison but apart from being used to cure severe headaches, it's used in face lifts; by injecting it you loosen your muscles and get rid of all the wrinkles in your face.

OK, I said to the doctor, but if all the wrinkles in my forehead will go away; how will I be able to carry out my job?

Don't my clients want to see me looking serious and worried?

Impact

Ten years ago I worked with a small publishing
company that published a lot of new Swedish
cartoons; it was fun and I tried to help them
with their finances.

One of their artists has moved south and when I
emailed him to order some books I asked if he
still remembered me, now ten years later.

By his answer I understood he recognized my
name but couldn't really place me and who I
was.

But later that day he mailed me again saying
that suddenly he had remembered me and he
wrote:

"..and you are the one who has a signed photo
of Jane Russell in your office"!

Who can forget a guy like me?

...Henry Denander

The study

The Board had decided to use a consultant to
make a study of our company and try to solve
all the problems we had within our big organization.

I was the chief financial officer struggling with
many problems and usually being the messenger
of all the bad news, since I was preparing
and presenting all the reports.

The day before the management consultants
arrived, the Managing Director (who was also
one of the owners) took me aside and prepared
me for all the criticism that I would face and
that I should not take it personally.

After one month, the study was done and the
preliminary report was presented but before it
could be shown to the Board some of the hardest
criticism was to be taken out because it became
too personal.

Anyway, the conclusion of the report was that we
had to employ a new Managing Director and
that the owner should separate himself from the
day-to-day business.

My department and I was of course were mentioned
many times but only with favorable comments
and the only advice given was that I needed more
resources – something I had demanded since I
started.

But I didn't take that personally.

Sumatra grass (1975)

Samosir Island on Lake Toba was said to be one of
the best places in the world for smoking grass and
I walked to the next village where the old woman in the
small restaurant was grinding some fresh coconut and
mixing it with oil and different weeds and she deep-fried it
all into delicious small cakes.

At first I didn't feel anything from the weed but after an
hour everything suddenly turned to color TV from the old
black & white and I walked down to my hut by the water
and took in all the sounds;

the waves from the Beethoven symphony, the singing
birds from Eric Satie's Gymnopédies, the sawing of the
wood from the Art Ensemble of Chicago and the chatting
at the nearby restaurant like in Bach's Motets.

Everything melted together in a mix of sensitive and
distinctive sounds and later I slept for an hour and woke
up and I was so hungry I rushed to the restaurant and
I couldn't stop eating.

No, I never smoked the wonderful Sumatra grass but
I had a wonderful coconut cake.

...Henry Denander

Interview

My friend The Waffle had read the long interview
with me in the American poetry magazine, and I
was interested to hear what he thought about it,
he's a book publisher and interested in poetry.

- Is it true what you said in the interview, he said;
that you don't drink anymore?

- Not even a beer? he said.

Maybe this is the thing that will make me
a famous poet?

Niagara Falls

My wife came back from a week-long
business trip to Canada, having been to
Toronto, Quebec and Montreal.

She was exhausted and jet-lagged
but over dinner she wanted to tell us
about her visit to the fantastic Niagara Falls.

During her long and vivid description of the
overwhelming and breathtaking sights,
I interrupted her, and told my son that
some people have even tried to
ride down the falls in a barrel!

- That would be easy for Homer Simpson
to do, my son answered. Ride down
the Niagara Falls in a barrel of Duff beer!

- I read once that Donald Duck went down
the falls in a barrell, I said. So maybe Homer
could do it as well!

My wife sighed and we could see that she was
really happy to be back home
in the real world again.

...Henry Denander

All blues

Miles Davis left Columbia Records
after 29 years and 44 albums and
moved to Warner Brothers;

"Twenty-nine years? Don't I get a
pension or something?",
Miles Davis said.

All my jobs

I first started working one really hot summer in
1962 delivering soft drinks from a truck in the
countryside outside my hometown Eskilstuna,
Sweden. I was ten years old and the driver was
from Denmark and I thought his way of speaking
Swedish was very exotic;

Then -
    there was a car rally not far from our summer
house and my friends and I sold programs and
stuck ads on all the cars. I remember the
ads for Canada Dry – a soft drink that never made
it here in Sweden. And I was really too shy to sell
programs;

Then -
    I worked as a postman on Saturdays in Eskilstuna,
while in high school - sharing a district with a good
friend. I remember those really early Saturday
mornings climbing all the stairs. This was at a time
when we still got mail on Saturdays and a time when
I could still easily run up three flights of stairs
without getting out of breath;

Then -
    I worked as a lathe operator every weekend while
in college, making taps for oil drums at a small
workshop. The manager was married to the owner's
daughter but still we made fun of the greedy old
man & I remember blood all over the floor and how I
almost lost the top of my thumb on one of those
dangerous machines;

...Henry Denander

Then -

I worked in a store in the very center of Stockholm
in the summer of 1972, selling refrigerators and spark
plugs. On the other side of the street was a bookstore
where I bought Neil Young's album Harvest and all
through the summer I played the song Heart of Gold;

Then -

I worked as a garbage man one summer. I hurt
my leg the first day on the job and I had to go to
the hospital to get stitches but I was back on the job
in the afternoon – this was a well paid job that
helped me get through the University and
I remember all the beer and soft drinks that
I brought home every day because people gave us
something for picking up their excess garbage;

Then -

I worked at the Arlanda airport cleaning the exterior
of airplanes at night all through University, until the
strong smell of the cleaning liquids made us all ill.
I remember the trip back home in the early morning,
all of us in the car tired and dizzy from the smells;

Then-
one summer I worked as a driver for a large
pharmaceutical company in Uppsala; a smooth
job in a VW van, cruising the University town.

Then -

I worked in the staff office at a large steelwork
outside Eskilstuna, keeping track of salaries for
two hundred employees who worked in shifts and

on a piece rate. Many years after I quit I could still
remember the employee numbers of some of the
workers when I saw them passing on the street;

Then -

I worked as a temporary teacher in college after I
finished University and it was strange since I was just
a few years older than my pupils;

Then -

I worked as a driver and telephone technician with
Ericsson in Melbourne, Australia and I learned the
tradition of drinking a lot of beer at lunch and taking
it really slowly in the afternoon;

Then -

I worked as painter for a month in Melbourne and
carefully and very slowly painted a whole health care
centre;

Then -

I worked in the financial department of the Ericsson
head office when I returned to Sweden in 1977, now
being a serious guy with a tie and no beer for lunch;

Then -

I was the financial manager of a large electrical
wholesaler for three years and learned a trade;

Then –

I worked as a financial manager for a Swedish
independent record company and paid out royalties
to U2, Paul Simon, Zoot Sims and Chet Baker;

...Henry Denander

And now –
for the last ten years I've had my own company
working as a business manager for Swedish artists.

Three years ago I started to write poetry and now
I try to remember what I have done all my life to
see if there was anything interesting to write a poem
about.

I have started with all my different jobs.

The next step will be to write the poem.

Synchronized Diving

While watching the Olympics I've seen
Synchronized Diving for the first time.

It's a fascinating sport; two divers doing exactly
the same dive, simultaneously and from diving
boards next to each other.

It's amazing how much training that must
go into this; they need to be extremely
skilled divers but then also practice the
synchronization.

Can you imagine how many times they've had
to get out of the cold pool and climb up the
stairs to the board? And then a quick dive and
up again.

I saw two brothers from Texas doing some
phenomenal dives together. I wonder how much
time their family has spent around the pool and
the diving boards.

In our family I think we'll stick to the
Synchronized Dining, it's hard enough to get
that working.

…Henry Denander

The cineaste

The film director Russ Meyer
has made some cult movies,
with classic titles like
"Faster Pussycat! Kill! Kill!" and
"SuperVIXENS".

His actresses seem to be cast after their
cup sizes and when he answered my letter
he had enclosed a signed photo of himself
holding a giant bra where he'd filled the
cups with two large melons.

I heard our young son asking his
mother about the Russ Meyer photo on our wall

- Ask your father, she said.

And, for once, I was the film expert
in the family.

Modern times

My doctor has given me
Botox and Zoloft to try to
relieve my headaches.

Botox is a common
ingredient when you do
facelifts and Zoloft is
one of the most common
anti-depressants.

I am a Modern Man; these are
the drugs of our times.

Only the Viagra is missing,
my wife said.

Nice try.

...Henry Denander

Standards in Norway, 1989

Keith Jarrett's Trio is playing
"Love Is A Many Splendoured Thing",
and Keith plays the E flat after the
drum solo.

On the second of the answering
syncopated accents,
there's a noticeable clam -
the "A" clashing with the "B flat".

Jarrett and Peacock didn't agree and
someone made a mistake.

Keith Jarrett, who is upset when
people in the audience are coughing or
clearing their throat –
wonder what he had to say about this?

Did he call the police?

Sapporo (The Sun Bear Concerts)

The beautiful first bars
of Keith Jarrett's solo concert;
improvised but crystal clear -
not even a cough from the audience
can destroy such a masterpiece.

...Henry Denander

untitled #3

I worked with the piano player
Romano Mussolini and
it was easy to get gigs in Italy
with a name like that in the band,
Chet Baker said.

Waiting for the line

I am leaning against the wall, reading the magazine I picked up
on the train. I'm watching the house on the other side of the street,
it's big and the door's impressive; the large stone inscription over the
door reads *Tag Members Only*, the stone looks very old, older than
the house itself. All the windows are barred and there is nothing
happening outside, no one entering or coming out. I am waiting for
the coffee shop to open and I will sit at the window table with my
note-book, where I have a good view of the house and its doorway.
I've been trying to write for months; I used to be able to jot down
ideas for poems all through the day, there was always something
grabbing my attention.

Here I am, across the street from the mansion-like building, ordering
coffee, staring out the window and checking the entrance. I know that
if I sit here long enough, everything will come back to me and slowly
I will see a line forming, outside The House of Tags.

...Henry Denander

Lunch at the castle

Every summer when I was a young boy we stayed in our summer house in the countryside outside Eskilstuna, a wonderful place for children, with a nice, long sandy beach not far from our cottage. Near the beach there was also an old castle, an enormous building, a huge house all in white where once the Swedish prince Eugen had lived. It was now a restaurant and a museum.

We only visited the restaurant once and, when we did, it was because some relatives came to visit, so my mother and I went there with my aunt and my cousin. The hallway coming into the castle was huge and impressive with a marble floor and stone walls. The restaurant was downstairs in the basement, with heavy dark walls and a very high ceiling. The old paintings on the walls were huge and almost as high as our cottage.

I was shy, as I was all through my childhood; I was maybe ten years old and not used to visiting restaurants, so the waiters and the large plates and the castle milieu made a strong impression on me.

So it was even more shocking and repulsive what happened after we had paid for the lunch, when my mother and aunt laughed and chuckled while they took the remains of the bread and the small packages of butter left on the table, and put them in their bags while the waiter was gone. Maybe it was the only thing I said during that lunch: "No, why are you doing this? You can't do that!"

I felt ashamed and embarrassed, like I was with poor people, taking the bread and the butter when the waiter wasn't watching, to bring home in a napkin in my aunt's bag.

Walking back home to the cottage after lunch, I wondered what it would be like to go to an ordinary restaurant with my relatives, if this was how they acted when they were eating at a castle.

A perfect client

My friend Rolf (The Waffle) called me and
begged me once more to help his old friend who
is a doctor and has started a small private practice
and needs some financial and administrative help.

When he called two months ago I said I was too
busy and I only work with entertainment clients but
this time I was persuaded to take him on as a client.

Ten minutes later the doctor called and he also
sent me an email with the financial details and
his questions. He also said I could call him anytime
on his mobile if I needed his medical advice.

This was before lunch.

Six hours later I am struck by a really painful attack
of kidney stones (it was ten years since this
happened the last time) and I suddenly realize I have
the telephone number to my new client, the doctor.

I call him and discover he is a surgeon and general
practitioner at the big hospital ten minutes from
where I live. He is there working and thirty minutes
later I meet him in the lobby and I get prescriptions
for painkillers and instructions of what to do.

The next day the pain is even worse and when I call
the doctor again (he is my client, you know) he is
working in the emergency unit. We meet there and
he puts me in a separate room and I get a VIP
treatment. All tests are done and all samples are

...Henry Denander

taken and in almost no time I am rushed off to be
X-rayed; I am taken care of by the huge resources of
the biggest hospital in Stockholm.

Hey,
I can actually take on a
few more clients
like this.

The Polish deli

The owner is grumpy and never smiles but
he has a wonderful apple cake.

He greets me and wants me to taste some sausages
and he's joking with the other customers and he
talks me into buying some ham – I was there for the
Apfelstrudel but there's none left.

He's loud and starts to talk about politics and
the reason why he, who has a University degree,
is selling sausages.

He describes the collapse of the Swedish system and
how our Prime Minister surrounds himself with
people that are not qualified for their jobs.

I realize he has been drinking and I can smell the
Slivovitz on his breath.

He doesn't want me to leave, he has solutions to
every problem in Sweden and when he starts talking
about Poland and their level of taxes on liquor, I
make a move for the door.

When I rush out he shouts after me:

- Will you come back?

Sure.

I love the Apfelstrudel.

...Henry Denander

A Serious Marriage

Why do you have to
take everything
so seriously?
I jokingly say
to my wife.
What do you
mean by that?
she answers.

The Doctor's patience

The record company I worked for made an
album with Johnny Winter and Dr. John,
and I took my friend Peter along to the
video recording of the gig.

When we met Dr. John backstage
my friend went straight up to him and
asked why he called himself "Doctor"
and the good Doctor looked like he
needed some very strong medicine.

...Henry Denander

Liverpool-Manchester United 1-2

The winter had not yet started
but I got a head cold that
made me spend two days in the sofa
in front of the new large screen TV

There was a Liverpool-Manchester United
soccer match in the afternoon
but I had a slight fever and when I woke up
I realized the match was already over

But it was OK, it was a rerun and I'd already
slept through that match the day before

Heavy drinking

I have almost stopped drinking now, perhaps a
beer once in a while in the summer and
some Retsina when I'm in Greece but not
the heavy drinking any more.

In the 80's I was out a lot and spent many nights in
restaurants and bars. It was a great time, funny things
happened and I met many interesting people.

But I am happy now without the heavy drinking – booze
makes me tired and the day after a late night out is a
disaster.

But of course, I have fond memories of the drinking and of
being drunk. I think of all the times I had a blackout and
the next day I couldn't remember what had happened after
3 AM.

I can't say I miss that.

But I have to admit
sometimes I even remember my blackouts
with affection.

...Henry Denander

It was not his fault

I'm listening to Joe Farrell and I remember the only time I've heard him before was when he was part of Chick Corea's Return To Forever, a band I listened to a lot once, maybe sometime in the early 70's. When I heard the music again later it sounded really dated and lightweight, tunes almost silly and Joe Farrell was playing flute on top of Corea's dancing piano. I didn't like it at all. But now when I hear Farrell from late 1985 - actually just four months before he died, only 48 years old, I wonder what happened - he plays a strong and fierce tenor saxophone, really good and powerful. It was probably not his fault, this Return to Forever band; probably it was all to blame on Mr. Corea.

The new sound of jazz

I read all afternoon, and also tried to sleep for a while with my music playing in the background, I listened to some jazz and when I was almost falling asleep I heard some strange trumpet blowing and it took me a while to grasp that it really was Miles Davis; it did not sound familiar and for once he seemed a bit lost. After listening to so many of his recordings I could hear his approach was different and that the sound of the band was different. I had to look up the notes from this concert and it turned out to be a radio broadcast from Stockholm in 1969. Chick Corea's electric piano had crashed and he had started out on the tune Bitches Brew with a malfunctioning electric piano. He managed to get the familiar sounds out of the instrument at first but slowly it started to sound like a cheap electric organ and this is probably what made Miles wander off with his trumpet, thinking about whether he should stop or not, but then he took it up again and the forceful drumming by Jack DeJohnette led the way when the piano was gone. After ten minutes Corea was back on an acoustic piano, not being able to add those layers of sound that was an important part of Miles's music at this stage, instead he was adding some block chords trying to build up the same sound. Because of the acoustic piano the band chose a different repertoire this evening at Folkets Hus Stockholm, and they played Paraphernalia, Nefertiti and Masqualero instead of the tunes from Bitches Brew. This is why my sleep was disturbed, thirty years later.

...Henry Denander

WIPE

I am submitting work to an Australian magazine called WIPE,
and all art should be on sheets of toilet paper.

I needed to find strong paper for this so I am buying
five different brands of Greek toilet paper rolls
in my local grocery store on the small Greek island.

Sofia in the store looks at my goods and smiles
and then she starts to laugh.

Then she says:
- Your family has left now?
- Yes, yes, I am here by myself this last week, I say.

She laughs again, and I wonder what she's thinking.
Her English is not perfect and my Greek is really bad so
I refrain from trying to explain what I was going to use the paper for.
It's not easy to explain anyway.

SELECTED POEMS

Just like that

I was exactly the same
when I was a child,
my wife says when our
six year old son does
something charming or
intelligent.

And every time he does
something stupid or does
not obey I ask my wife if
she was also like that
when she was a child.

And I know what
she will say.

Call The Police

When we moved in to this flat our upstairs
neighbor still had his three teenage kids living
with him, since then the children have moved out
and it's very quiet.

They had a lot of parties and were sometimes
really loud. The father was on tour in the summer
and every weekend there was a party upstairs.

But we never complained, they were dancing and
singing and for us there was no real problem.
They were always really kind and well behaved –
just young and happy. The father asked me once
if there was a problem when he was away and I
never grumbled, only told him that please if he
could hide that trumpet when he leaves next time.

One evening I went up there to protest but it was
not a party it was the son Calle playing his
electric guitar with the amplifier extremely loud
and his room was right above our bedroom.

One morning I met Calle and his sister in the lift
and we talked about everything but never
mentioned the party they had last weekend.

Suddenly Calle said:

– I can hear you snoring from below, you must be
snoring really loud.

...Henry Denander

- Yes, perhaps I do, I said.

I realized I have been too kind to them, I should have been more militant. They have no respect for me. Next time I will call the police.

Before they do.

How to draw like Picasso

In my spare time I have been trying to
draw portraits, from photos of jazz
musicians and writers.

After many failures I found that my
talent in drawing was knowing when to
stop; I left all the complicated things
out of my drawings.

Picasso said that after learning to draw
professionally he spent a lifetime trying
to draw like a child.

I took a shortcut and went straight to
the children's style, without passing
through art school.

...Henry Denander

The poetry of Tax Declarations

On my way home from the office today, traveling
on bus number 66, I scribbled down a poem on the
back of a tax declaration form.

I have been doing tax declarations for my clients
for two months now. Soon I will have prepared over
a hundred of them.

A friend told me he knew of some famous poets who
had ordinary jobs but wrote poetry at their spare time.

William Carlos Williams was a doctor and wrote
poems on the back of prescriptions between patients.

Wallace Stephens worked for an insurance company and
ended up as a vice president.

TS Eliot was a teacher and a bank clerk before he started
to work for a publisher.

On the back of the tax declaration form I wrote a poem
about a client and a negotiation I had just finalized and
about how upset I had been with the other party for trying
to fool me and my client.

I know that Elliot and Stevens never wrote about their day
jobs but William Carlos Williams wrote poems and stories
about his patients and cases.

And he could call himself a doctor and a poet
at the same time.

Is it possible to be a bean
counter
and a poet
at the same time?

Probably depends on the
poetry,
not on the job.

...Henry Denander

headache & a cup of coffee

keith jarrett is fingering away
some well known melodies
all by himself
more controlled than he usually is
hesitating to take off without the bass
and the drums
perhaps waiting for them
to arrive

trying to get the guts to go to the office
and do some work this Saturday but i´ve got a headache and
i ended up in front of the computer

my wife and young son are visiting the Mother-in-law
over the weekend
i will call them later
tell them i have been working all day

i am surfing on the net and sending emails and answering letters and
writing a long poem
about the time i met chet baker in london
in 1986

making a cup of coffee from the greek coffee that we brought home
from hydra
it´s nescafé but in the greek way

tastes great
stir it into hot milk and you are
in java paradise

it started to snow again yesterday
bad news

now it´s five in the afternoon and
still light outside
i think the winter
will slowly leave now

thinking of writing a poem about just nothing
or perhaps about the things i have been doing today

i´ll think about it

we'll see

…Henry Denander

Bus # 66

We live on one of the islands in the center of
Stockholm and my office is not far away; it takes
me about twenty minutes to get there in the morning.

I am overweight and have high blood pressure and
my doctor thinks it's a good idea for me to walk to
the office every day.

But I usually take bus # 66, it stops just ten meters
from our house and when I get off at my office I only
have fifty meters to walk.

Before the summer they suddenly moved the bus stop
outside our building, fifty meters up the street.

And when I came back from the summer I noticed
they had also moved the bus stop at my office;
now I have to walk at least three hundred meters.

It feels like they are after me and I suspect that my
doctor is involved in this.

But, Dr. Gillgren, just to let you know:

From now on I am taking the
subway instead.

The White Album

I was going to order a bunch of records and
I called the distribution centre that handles all
the Swedish record companies (as we work in
the entertainment field we have an account there).

The woman who dealt with my order excused herself,
she was new and it took some time for her to handle
the computer. Everything was fine, I didn't mind but,
when I ordered a copy of The Beatles' White Album,
she couldn't find it:

-Did you say Beatles? The Wide Album..? She was
not sure.

I tried to control myself not being clever and witty but
I said it was The White Album, not The Wide Album,
and in the end she had some help from a colleague and
of course they found the album.

And she told me the title was not The White Album,
that's just what people call it. It doesn't have a title and
that's the reason she couldn't find it.

I didn't comment, I realized I was on thin ice.

Instead I just ordered a copy of
The Beatles' album Sergeant Popper and
a Boothoven piano concert.

...Henry Denander

The salmon in the sky and how everything just stopped

No one died but a few people were injured and it was
a miracle that it didn't end in a disaster since Stockholm was
    filled with hundreds of thousands of people. It was
The Water Festival and there were crowds of people
    everywhere; on bridges, on the islands and
        all over the city.

Strangely enough, someone's brainless idea of showing the
newest Swedish fighter jet and flying it over Stockholm had
    somehow been approved.

I stayed at home since I hated the crowds but when I heard
    the loud noise from the plane's engine I walked out on the
balcony and saw a very impressive JAS 32 fly over
    our house.

Then when the plane disappeared over the roofs of the
    houses on the other side of the street suddenly
everything turned quiet. When I looked up I glimpsed
the plane turning up towards the sky and after the
    engine stopped everything was so quiet, as though
the whole city had just stopped and everyone was waiting
        for the plane to crash.

It was more than ten years ago and the feeling of someone
        just turning off the sound of the city,
    and the plane in the sky,
like a small salmon in a rushing water, showing its belly
    and struggling in the sun,

                that's what I remember.

Old and new songs

My wife's standard comment when she hears a new hit song on the radio is that it reminds her of another song.

I argue that if you listen one more time to the song it will have its own qualities and it's fashionable to use licks and hooks from old songs. Remember Mozart was inspired by many other compositions. And Bach used known melodies in his works as well.

A lot of my clients are composers but only once have I been involved in a proper dispute regarding a song.

And the Assessment Committee voted in our favor; my client's song was not stolen from someone else's song.

I am glad my wife was not on that Committee.

...Henry Denander

A record and a letter

It was 1982 and I was sitting in my office
trying to balance the books of the company
I worked for.

They call
me from the record store: "Hey,
your Bukowski record has arrived!"

I had forgotten about this, ordered
the record over a year ago.

I picked it up; the store was in the centre
of Stockholm. The record looked really good
Bukowski wearing his jacket the wrong way.
On Takoma.

(Two years later when I was working for
this big Swedish Record company
distributing the Takoma label I could say: "Hmm,
Takoma, I know about them, they
have some good stuff...".)

From the record store I drove the small car
to my flat on the south side of town. Over the bridges.
Cold but no snow on the streets.
Always rain.

When I opened the door
with the Buk record in my hand
there was this letter on
the floor, sender Bukowski, San Pedro.

I remember
I wrote Buk after reading
Factotum, six months ago.

Bukowski wrote that he was happy that
his books worked for me.

These things
made me
feel honored in some
strange way.

...Henry Denander

Life and death in the bowling alley

I hadn't bowled for at least twenty
years but I used to be really good
and my wife and son talked me into
trying it again and after
my first three strikes I got carried
away and I made a mistake and one
finger got so badly twisted I
couldn't finish the game.

Now three weeks later
my index finger is still swollen and
blue and hurting and I had to get it
x-rayed to see if it was broken.

While I was waiting at the
hospital I realized this was
the prize I had to pay for
trying to beat the shit out of
my seven year old son and
his mother on her birthday.

Accept your name

Henry Chesney Baker
and Henry Charles Bukowski;

if I had known about these guys when
I was young perhaps I would have liked
my own name better.

My name is OK now but I was never very
pleased with it when I was a kid.

At that time no one here in
Sweden knew about Chet or Buk
but now it's good to be able to
tell people that both of them were
named Henry.

And no one needs to know that
Buk never liked Henry
but used Charles instead.

...Henry Denander

Via Formia

At the train station in Naples we
notice that the next train to
Rome travels via Formia and
that's were we want to get off.

This was better than we thought,
two hours and we
will be there.

On the way on the train we
are paying for our tickets and
we discover that the train will go
directly to Rome.

But, we say, it said "Via Formia" on the
big sign.

Yes, the train will pass Formia but
it will not stop there.

We had to go all the way to Rome and
then back again.

This is charming when you are on holiday but
this would never happen here in Sweden,
of course.

But here in Sweden there is no
place called Formia,
only places like Eskilstuna and Nässjö,
where trains seldom stop anyway.

The SASE

On eBay I bought a self-addressed and
stamped envelope that the poet Charles Bukowski
sent to Chiron Review in the 80's.

This is the system, you send poems to a
magazine or a publisher and if they like them
they will use the SASE to reply to you.

More likely they will not use your poems and
return them in the SASE with a brief standard note
telling so.

Many poets have written about how they received
their first rejection letter or how they have their
drawers full of rejection slips.

Even Bukowski got rejection slips. In the early days.

I have framed the Bukowski envelope and
it looks nice on my wall.

It's a nice conversation piece; when someone asks
about it I tell them the story of how it works and also,
sort of by the way,
I tell them that Chiron Review is
actually the magazine where I had my
first poem published.

And I don't mention any of my
rejection letters.

...Henry Denander

The Champ

The boxing match was on the radio and we
got up in the middle of the night to listen.

It was 1959 and I was seven years old and
we were in our little summer house outside of
Eskilstuna. My father and I sat close to the
Blaupunkt transistor radio, listening to how
Ingemar Johansson won over Floyd Patterson and
how we got a Swedish Champ.

"My brother's name was also Henry",
Ingemar Johansson said, thirty years later, when
I met him late one night in a bar. He told me about
his brother who had been ill and died young.

He was signing an autograph for me with the
nice big expensive ink pen I always carried.

"When I was a kid in Gothenburg, I found a
pen like this on the street", he said.

Suddenly I was reminding him of *his* childhood.

"One more beer for the Champ, please!"

Wormwood Review

For my fiftieth birthday
I bought myself a full run
of Wormwood Review,
the little magazine that
started in the 1960's and
put out 144 issues of poetry
for nearly forty years.

I have many poet friends in
America who talk about
when they had a poem published in
WR and how much the late
editor Marvin Malone meant
to them.

Charles Bukowski said that
this was the best U.S.
poetry magazine and that it was run by a
no bullshit editor.

One of my good friends said in
a letter: As you know, in
purchasing that full run of
Wormwoods you acquired the
best single repository of
American poetry from the
second half of the twentieth
century.

...Henry Denander

Today in the mail I received the
box from America.

144 issues filled with poetry.

Is it too early to retire?

Condoms at the airport

While changing planes in Vienna
I took my son to the Men's room
and he asked me about the condom
dispenser on the wall.

"I don't know, maybe it's soap or
something," I said.

I didn't feel the time and the place
was right for going through these
matters with my eight year old son,

"No, it's not soap", he said, "and it
says LOVE on them."

We had to rush to the plane and he
dropped his investigation.

Soon I will have to explain these
matters for him, though.

But if he knows about LOVE
already, maybe it will be easy to
explain the rest.

...Henry Denander

footsteps

at six in the morning I am
wakened by donkeys passing
outside

in the narrow stone paved
street

on their way
down to the port.

i hear
chickens and
a rooster from the garden
next door.

it is
easy to
go back
to

sleep.

Ghikas & the razor

Ghikas commented on my long beard when
I entered his grocery store; I said it had
grown too long to shave and I needed to go to the barber
to have it cut.

But he said he had a razor that would work and showed
me the Bic Metal Plus T7.

After I'd paid for everything he told me that every time
he slaughters a pig he shaves it with one of these razors,
it's the only one that works.

We both laughed and I could hear him laughing even
after I'd left the store.

In the evening when we walked by,
I was clean-shaven and we were heading
down to the port for dinner.

"You look nice", Ghikas said when we passed.

I was flattered.

...Henry Denander

7 AM at the Zeus hotel

Because of a long swim in the sun yesterday and
a three-hour long siesta in the afternoon, I wake up
before 7 AM this morning.

I sneak out of the room and take a table at the front
of the hotel, overlooking the beach. No one else is
around, no guests, only Paris Theodorakidis and
his dog Astero.

Paris gets me a cup of coffee and Astero leans her
head on my leg. The small city of Tolo starts to
wake up, there are deliveries of Loutraki water,
fish, fruit and vegetables. Some early swimmers
are heading down to the beach.

After a while Paris gives me an omelet and some
bread.

I have my notebook and the book on Mycenae, I
drink coffee, pat the dog and write some stuff in
my notebook.

Stuff like this.

Early morning at Ghikas'

I don't drink wine or stronger
stuff these days, I only get tired and the day
after drinking is killing me but the first
night on our Greek island at the Taverna
Kristina I got carried away and had far too
much Retsina
and I woke up in the middle
of the night with anguish and pains in my
chest and a throbbing heart and I couldn't
go back to sleep and in the morning I felt
horrible and when I stumbled up to Ghikas'
to get some fresh bread I met the island
doctor with four men carrying a stretcher
with the corpse of a man who had just died
only sixty years old
and Ghikas was sad as he
knew the man who lived just around the
corner and he used to come to the shop
every day but this morning his heart had
just stopped
and I took a loaf of the warm,
fresh bread that Ghikas had just brought on
his donkey from the bakery in the port
and I walked back to our
house of course realizing I'd probably never
drink again

...Henry Denander

Neeli Cherkovski at the Bratsera Hotel

There was a poster announcing Neeli Cherkovski
reading his poetry at the Bratsera Hotel on Hydra.

We'd never met but we have some common
friends and we are both in books coming out of
12 Gauge Press and Bottle of Smoke Press in
America so I went by to say hello and we had a
nice chat.

The crowd of expatriates on this small Greek
island had showed up at the reading and the
well-known American painter came up to
talk – I know him a little and he knows
I am a bean counter from Sweden.

You two know each other? he said when Neeli
and I were talking.

Yeah, we are both poets and we have the same
publisher in America, I said

and I tried to sound really relaxed and like it was
the most natural thing in the world.

Henry's view

Henry Miller passed the island of Poros on his way to
Hydra in 1939 and from the boat he could see straight
into the houses of the Greek families.

Over the years I have always looked at the port of
Poros from the ferryboat trying to catch this view and
today, coming really close to land I suddenly saw the
three story house with the big balcony doors and at
the far end of the big room I saw an old woman on a
chair looking out at the ship.

Here it was at last, the view from The Colossus of
Maroussi: the boat sailing through the streets of
Poros, the old house, the big room and it could be the
same woman now 64 years older.

Maybe she was looking for Henry the same way
I was looking for her.

...Henry Denander

My Funny Valentine

The first flat of my own in Stockholm was
really small but in a nice area on one of
the islands south of the old town.

My girlfriend often stayed with me,
since her own flat was way out
in the suburbs.

The two of us never rang the
doorbell but used
the squeaking mail slot in the door;
when it was opened slowly it made a sound that
could be heard in the flat
and made you rush to the door.
You knew who was there.

Years later, we have been
married for some time,
having dinner in our new flat
listening to a recording of
Miles Davis
playing at Philharmonic Hall in New York
in 1964.

My Funny Valentine

Suddenly, half way into the song,
we both look up and listen,
Miles Davis is improvising and

playing a
long
single
note
the exact
tone
of that
squeaking mail slot

We smile
and feel proud
to share
this small secret
with Miles.

...Henry Denander

Jerry Jeff Walker at Mosebacke

My friend Ake and I left the big
release party and took a taxi to
Mosebacke, a small music club in
the south of Stockholm.

Jerry Jeff Walker was playing there,
alone with his guitar. He had just started
when we entered the small bar, it was
absolutely quiet and everyone was
listening carefully.

He was one of my heroes from the time I
first started to listen to singer/songwriters in
the sixties; Tom Paxton, Gordon Lightfoot,
Tom Rush and Leonard Cohen, of course.

Ake and I were standing there in the bar
with a beer and it was one of those gigs
were you felt no need to talk, just smile.
Jerry Jeff had written so many classic songs and
he had us all under his spell.

In the intermission he was standing
there in the bar having a beer and I got him to
sign me an autograph and I cleared my voice
and said that he had written one of the best
songs ever written, "More Often Than Not",
on that album from the late sixties.

- Well, I actually didn't write that song, it was
written by David Wiffen, he said.

I felt like a fool of course, but later on stage he
said he was going to do a song he hadn't
done in a long time and there it was, this beautiful
song, with just Jerry Jeff Walker's voice, his guitar
and no other comments.

…Henry Denander

Mr. J.C.

John William Coltrane died
of liver failure,
on July 17, 1967.

Four days later
Albert Ayler played at
his funeral at St. Peter's
Lutheran Church in New York.

And in Oslo they
were marching
down Karl Johan,
protesting against
his death.

Patrons are requested to keep as quiet as possible during the artistes performance

The Portobello Hotel was on a nice,
quiet street,
this was before the Notting Hill area
got so famous and busy.

The guy in the reception
looked up at me and said:
"A guy called Chet phoned for you".
There was a note for me.

The night before, my friend Lars and I had been to
Ronnie Scott's.
Chet Baker was playing there with
his band.

We met Chet Baker before the gig and I gave him a
copy of a video that was made in Stockholm some
months before.
The record company I worked for had
made a record with Chet and this was
the video.

I don't think he remembered me
from Stockholm.
I was the one that paid him his royalties but he
had been given many royalty checks in his time.
But he was nice and we
talked briefly and I said that we would come to the gig
the next day also.

It was a great gig, that first night, Chet and the band were
tight. Chet's voice was strong and weak in the right
way.

…Henry Denander

Played the trumpet like no one else. Only he could sound like that.
A great gig.

The telephone message said:
Chet phoned.
"We would like to come and
have a chat with you
at the hotel.
We'll arrive before 10 PM
tonight"

I was stunned – Chet wanted to come by to see us.

But in the afternoon I was busy working and
we heard nothing more from Chet.
Later I met up with Lars and we went to Langan's Brasserie for
a long dinner. We met some people there and
after some bar visits we went back to Ronnie Scott's.

We were in a really good mood and we
met more people there at the bar.
And lots of drinks were ordered.
We had a few games of poker dice and
we were not paying full attention
to the band.

There were people telling us
to stop talking and laughing.
And someone showing us a sign saying
the audience should be
quiet
during the
performance.

Anyway, Lars and I had a great time and we
stayed for the whole set and ended up
taking a nightcap in the
downstairs bar at Portobello Hotel at about
3.30 in the morning.

Suddenly three more people stumbled
in to the otherwise quiet bar.
Chet Baker and his flute player Nicola Stilo
and their manager
coming straight from Ronnie Scott's.

The party started over again.
We order more drinks.
Chet is slowly sipping shots of Amaretto
with ice.
We sit and talk. Chet tells about their
recent tour in Japan, where they were really
popular. Lots of people at the
concerts. Like a pop band.

Suddenly they all started discussing the Ronnie Scott's gig,
how great it was to
play there but tonight was bad because the
audience was so loud and noisy.
They all agreed with this and Lars and I just
nodded and said, "Yeah, right" and tried to
talk more about Japan or Sweden
or the like.

I didn't dare look at Lars because we would probably
start to laugh.

...Henry Denander

The flute player went on and on about the
noisy crowd but
in the end we went on to talk about
something else.

They were apparently not aware they were
talking to
the two loudest
troublemakers
in the
audience.

We had some more beers. Chet ordered another
Amaretto with ice.
Perhaps he was on or off drugs and needed the
sweet drink?

At six in the morning we all hugged and they left in a cab.

The guy in the bar came up.
That was Chet Baker, wasn't it?
Yeah, right, I said.
Like it was the most natural thing in the world.

We never saw them again.
And two years later Chet was gone,
flying from the window
of that hotel
in Amsterdam.

So what

I read an interview with Miles Davis
and he said he had never turned his back to
the audience trying to be cool or tough,
it was just because he wanted to hear the
high notes and to direct the band.

So - when he came on stage in Stockholm
in 1973 and he was spitting on the floor
in front of 2,000 people, maybe it was just to
clear his throat?

And when he walked off stage after his
solos - it was probably because he got a
phone call or something.

...Henry Denander

Chet Baker at Fasching

Chet Baker came to Stockholm to play the Fasching Jazz Club. He called and I went to see him at his hotel. We had spent some time together in London the year before and he was one of my jazz heroes.

At the Salvation Army hotel I was shown to his room but Chet hardly wanted to open the door, he just took the recordings I brought him and we chatted briefly. He had a friend in there, a Swedish jazz musician and the hotel room was filled with sweet and heavy smoke. I left and we said we would talk more at the jazz club that night.

In between sets at Fasching I tried to get in contact with Chet but his friend was really nervous and the same sweet smoke came out of Chet's dressing room. I said hi to Chet & his band but soon the Swedish friend closed the door.

I was the financial director of Chet's record company in Sweden; I was a bean counter but not a police officer. Chet knew this, we had been drunk together in London, but his friend from Sweden maybe thought I was with the drug enforcement agency.

I left them and went back to my friends at the bar and got drunk on beer and Jaegermeister.

Chet's playing that night at Fasching was absolutely beautiful, the tone of his trumpet and voice was so very soft and he sounded better than ever.

Or maybe it was just because we were
high, Chet and I?

Late night philosophy

People from the 70's
are not what they
used to be when I was
young, my wife said.

Well, I think they say
the same things
about you, I said.

...Henry Denander

XXL

I have lost 20 pounds and I am very pleased with
myself.

My son can't understand the difference though, he still thinks
I am fat. I realized that today when we walked down the
street.

William has started to read and he is keen on reading the
registration numbers of cars passing – to see if the first three
letters form a funny word. He is also getting interested in
cars.

Ten years ago when we moved to a new flat in the centre of
Stockholm we sold our car and we've been going by taxi the
few times we needed to go somewhere where the bus or
subway couldn't take us.

William now realizes that all his friends' parents have cars
and what he thought was the luxury of riding a taxi once in a
while is now overshadowed by friends getting picked up at
school in nice looking cars.

- "Dad, if you bought a new car..," he said.

- "Yeah…"

- "I am sure the registration number would begin with XXL".

live at the village vanguard

i had listened many times to art pepper's beautiful
recording from 1975 before i saw the photo taken
back stage on that thursday night at the village
vanguard;

he seemed to be on drugs and he looked pale and
scary and totally gone

i can't say i could hear his pain but the next time
i listened to "but beautiful" and "valse triste"
they sounded very different

and even the tempo

had changed

...Henry Denander

Birthday bowling

Our son wanted to go bowling on his
birthday and in the middle of the
game my wife said I should take it
easy and let William win –
so I slipped a couple of times and
threw a few balls down the gutter.

Suddenly I realized my wife was
playing like she always did, and after
two more strikes she was winning and
I finished up last behind William.

When I protested afterwards my wife
wondered if it was *me* that was
turning eight today.

How to write a poem

When I'm relaxed & not stressed by work and
I'm feeling well and balanced, it's easy to get
ideas for poems.

I try to write about almost anything;

the weather or just making observations on
people passing on the street or what goes on
in my head while having a cup of coffee down at
Café Merci on Hornsgatan;

But these days my poems are full of
complaints and annoying ideas of
how much better everything used to be.

Just like this poem.

I wish I could write a poem about the
small fly that circles over the head of
the pretty schoolgirl at the table
next to me.

But not this time.

...Henry Denander

A healthy man (backstage at The Fasching Jazz Club)
For Dag and Rune

A group of us were celebrating Father's Day at the
Café Opera and it was just one of those days when
everyone was in the mood for a party, so we started
drinking at a high tempo - beer and champagne and
wine and a lot of different shots.

Someone reminded us that Chet Baker was playing at
the Fasching Jazz Club and we ought to go there and
say hello; we all worked for a Swedish independent
record company and we'd recorded an album with him
that summer.

We stumbled into the club just in time to hear the
last tune and when we came into his dressing room,
Chet looked at us and laughed and thanked
us all for coming.

Chet, who was the model of a drug addicted jazz
musician, looked like he was in better shape than we
were.

No wonder he had chosen to record for our company.

The last stanza

I had a letter from a magazine editor saying he
passed on my poems, which is fine of course, but
in the end he added that he really liked one of my
poems up to the last stanza which he didn't like
at all.

I liked the letter from the editor
except *his* last stanza.

...Henry Denander

A SHORT STORY

The poetry of Mr. Blue

The sun is rising over the lemon tree in Athanasia's garden next door, I'm having some yoghurt with fresh figs and honey, reading the last pages of Paul Auster's book "The Brooklyn Follies", when there is a light knock on the door and young Yannis brings me a letter that had been delivered to the grocery store last night.

This is odd since my mail is always delivered to my box at the post office down in the harbor here on Hydra. I open the envelope to find a handwritten note from Harold White, one of the painters on the island. I don't know Mr. White personally but I know who he is and I've seen some of his beautiful water colors. He writes he wants to meet me, to talk and show me some of his paintings. I'm surprised, it would be great to meet him.

When I call the number he's given me later, there's only a machine saying that Harold White is in America for the summer and messages can be left with Mrs. Kalovradi.

It takes me some time to find her but that night when I eventually do find her, she is in her art gallery, in one of the alleys leading down to the port.

- Oh, I'm sorry. You didn't know? she says. Harold White died earlier this summer. He was buried in San Francisco last week.

This is a shock, I just had a letter from him. I look up and I see all the paintings in the gallery. There are more than twenty watercolors, all by Harold White.

- He didn't even get to see his paintings hanging here in the gallery, she says. He died just before the exhibition opened.

Suddenly I realize that what I'm looking at is a beautiful painting of the artist Ghikas' old house, the way it looked before it was destroyed in the fire in 1960. I am fascinated by this house and all the stories about Ghikas and about when Henry Miller visited him on Hydra. I even wrote a poem about it earlier this summer.

The next painting makes me stop, it's almost abstract, but I instantly see what it is, it's Henry Miller and Ghikas playing ping-pong in 1939. I wrote about this in a poem this summer. It must be a coincidence!

Mrs. Kalovradi asks me if I live here on Hydra and I introduce myself and tell her I have a house in Kamini.

- Oh, you are Mr. Blue!? she says. Harold talked a lot about you.

This confuses me even more since I never even said "hi" to him when I passed him on the steps going up and down to the port. Maybe he had read one of my poetry collections? I must ask her but I have to see all his paintings first. In a strange way it seems like he had been interested in a lot of the same things as I have.

And the more I see, the more connections I find to things I've written this summer, I become really perplexed. I find painting after painting with titles or motives that are based on the poems I've written. It feels like I'm in a vacuum, everything else around me has stopped and is erased and gone.

No one else has read these latest poems of mine! No one except my friend Harry van Layden, who's another painter living on the island. But he's not on speaking terms with White, apparently they had an argument over a beautiful Scandinavian girl some years ago and they haven't spoken since.

...Henry Denander

I feel weak. I ask Mrs. Kalovradi for some water. She gives me a glass and I make myself ask her when White made these paintings. She says he painted them all in July this year. He was in his studio almost day and night.

I understand that she had worked as his secretary, I wonder if they had been lovers; the way she talked about Harold made me think they had been very close. She says I could talk to Despina Aspro, the young girl who has been his assistant in the studio. She knows much more about the paintings, if I'm interested.

Mrs. Kalovradi calls Despina and I arrange to meet her next morning, down at Giorgios' Café in the port.

That night I have problems getting to sleep, I think about the paintings and the letter from Harold White, delivered weeks after his death – maybe there is a simple explanation to the letter but I can't understand how he had been able to read the twenty poems I had written. I really like coincidences but this is too much. It just wasn't possible and even if ideas and gossip travel quickly around Hydra, he would've had to break in to my house to read my poetry.

The next morning I am early for my meeting with Despina Aspro. The sun isn't hot yet and there is a nice breeze. I see her coming from the far end of the port, heading straight at me in her bare feet on the old stones. She is a beautiful Greek woman, maybe in her early twenties, with long dark hair and beautiful clear blue eyes. She moves like she is completely unaware of her looks, unconscious of how the thin cotton dress shows her beautiful young body.

She kisses me on both cheeks in the typical Greek way when we introduce ourselves. She looks like a Greek Princess. I wonder how she could have known it was me?

-I saw that it was you, even with your new beard, she says and laughs.

-Harold told me so much about you, she says. I've really been looking forward to meet you. I love your writing!

I am flattered, of course, and I can't help staring at her. She is maybe half my age but I realize she makes me nervous, she's such a natural beauty.

Still I wonder if it's all a setup, a large scale practical joke. Is there a camera somewhere, making a fool of me for a whole audience. Is this beautiful girl a fan of me and my writing? Are Harold White's paintings a reality and had he really been able to read my poems? Or is it just me, reading too many Paul Auster books this summer?

We talk about ourselves. She tells me a bit about her art school and she asks me about my books. After a while I start questioning her about White's paintings. I ask her if she was with him this summer in the studio, when he painted for the exhibition.

Despina suddenly gets up to leave, she says she has to go back to the studio. I can't understand why she has to leave so soon; I suggest we meet again tonight for dinner, I am desperate to see her soon again and I want to know the story behind the paintings.

- I can't, she says, I'm going to San Francisco tomorrow morning, my father is getting buried this weekend.

- Your father?

...Henry Denander

- Yes, Harold White was my father. Didn't you know that?

- No. I am really sorry to hear this, I am sorry about your loss. Mrs. Kalovradi didn't say that Harold White was your father, but she said that he has been buried already.

- Incredible! You shouldn't believe anything that witch says! Despina says, looking really upset.

Despina gives me her telephone number, she's not coming back to Hydra until next month. Call me later this afternoon, she says. She kisses me lightly on the mouth and rushes off, taking one of the small lanes up from the port, heading towards White's studio.

I order a frappé and a chocolate croissant and stare out over the sea, even more confused than before. After an hour I call her number but there's an answering machine stating that Harold and Despina White are in America and will be back in January.

I wonder if this is just an oversight, leaving an old message on the machine. Or is the message on the machine true? There's no logic in anything. Why did she rush off, we had barely met?

When I pass Mrs. Kalovradi's gallery on the way back to my house, the shop is closed, the windows are barred and all the posters from the exhibition are gone. A small printed sign on the door says the gallery will open again in January next year, with an exhibition by Harold White called "The new poetry of Mr. Blue".

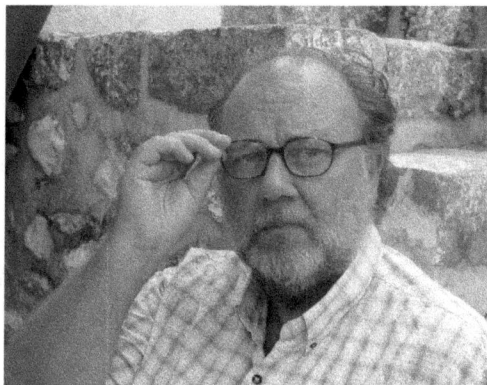

HENRY DENANDER was born in 1952 and
lives in Stockholm, Sweden and on Hydra Island
in Greece. For over 25 years he has worked on the
business side of the entertainment industry. He is
also the editor of Kamini Press.

Henry Denander's books are *I know What She Will
Say* (Bottle of Smoke Press, 2003), *Weeks Like This*
(Bottle of Smoke Press, 2005), *Bring Down The Sun*
(ArtBureau, 2005), *The Poetry of Mr. Blue* (Bottle
of Smoke Press, 2007), *The Loulaki Bar* (Miskwabik
Press, 2009).

His first poem was published in 1999 and now
he's had over two hundred poems and many
illustrations published in small press magazines and
on the web. He's been published mainly in America
but also in places like Belgium, New Zealand,
Australia, India and the UK. He has a website with
poetry and art at **www.henrydenander.com**

ABOUT THE LUMMOX PRESS

LUMMOX PRESS was created in 1994 by RD Armstrong. It began as a self-publishing/DIY imprint for poetry by RD. Several chapbooks were published and in late 1995 Lummox began publishing the Lummox Journal, a monthly small/underground press lit-arts mag. Available primarily by subscription, the LJ continued its exploration of the "creative process" until its demise as a print mag in 2006. It was hailed as one of the best monthlies in the small press by John Berbrich and Todd Moore.

In 1998, Lummox began publishing the Little Red Book series, and continues to do so today. To date there are some 60 titles in the series and a collection of poems from the first decade of the series has been published under the title, The Long Way Home (2009); it's a great way to explore the series.

Together with Chris Yeseta (Layout and Art Direction since 1997), RD continues to publish books that are both striking in their looks as well as their content…published because of the merit of the work, not the fame of the author. That's why there are so many first full-length collections in the roster (look for the *).

The following books are available directly from the Lummox Press via its website: **www.lummoxpress.com** or at Lummox c/o PO Box 5301, San Pedro, CA 90733. There are also E-Book (PDF) versions of most titles available. Most of these titles are available through other book sellers online, as well.

The Wren Notebook by Rick Smith (2000)
Last Call: The Legacy of Charles Bukowski
  edited by RD Armstrong (2004)
On/Off the Beaten Path by RD Armstrong (2008)
Fire and Rain—Selected Poems 1993-2007 Volumes 1 & 2
  by RD Armstrong (2008)*

El Pagano and Other Twisted Tales by RD Armstrong
   (short stories—2008)*
New and Selected Poems by John Yamrus (2009)
The Riddle of the Wooden Gun by Todd Moore (2009)
Sea Trails by Pris Campbell (2009)
Down This Crooked Road—Modern Poetry from the Road
   Less Traveled edited by RD Armstrong and
   William Taylor, Jr. (2009)
The Long Way Home edited by RD Armstrong (2009)
Drive By by John Bennett (2010)
Modest Aspirations by Gerald Locklin & Beth Wilson (2010)
Steel Valley by Michael Adams (2010)*
Hard Landing by Rick Smith (2010)
A Love Letter to Darwin by Jane Crown (2010)*
E/OR—Living Amongst the Mangled by RD Armstrong (2010)
Ginger, Lily & Sweet Fire a cookbook
   by H. Lamar Thomas (2010)*
Whose Cries Are Not Music by Linda Benninghoff (2011)*
Dog Whistle Politics by Michael Paul (2011)*
What Looks Like an Elephant by Edward Nudleman (2011)*
Working the Wreckage of the American Poem
   edited by RD Armstrong (2011)
Living Among the Mangled (revised) by RD Armstrong,
   special edition, (2011)
The Accidental Navigator by Henry Denander (2011)*
Catalina by Laurie Soriano (2011)*

www.ingramcontent.com/pod-product-compliance
Lightning Source LLC
Chambersburg PA
CBHW071131090426
42736CB00012B/2088